Walk Fast, Talk Loud and Smile

Think Big!

To order additional copies, please contact us.
BookSurge, LLC
www.booksurge.com
1-866-308-6235
orders@booksurge.com

DAVID OTIS

WALK FAST, TALK LOUD AND SMILE

How to Succeed in Sales and Have Fun Doing It

2006

Walk Fast, Talk Loud and Smile

CONTENTS

Dear Readers,

Congratulations! You have made a potentially life changing decision. Walk Fast! Talk Loud! And Smile! It sounds too easy to be true. In fact most of the sales concepts that David speaks about in his book are neither that technical nor hard to execute. That is why anyone can take these fundamentals and use them to enhance their God given talents and abilities to succeed in a sales career.

My name is Jeremy Wood, and in August of 2003, I started my career in sales. My first experience in sales was a very stressful and uneasy time in my career. I had to get out of my comfort zone and make some bold moves for my future. My sales manager, David Otis, I started with spoke daily of how our attitude and sales skills combined with a consistent self development routine would jump start my sales achievements. He was correct! Although I resisted using these methods early on, I reluctantly gave in SINCE my way was not working. David had a system and a method that he guaranteed would give me success. I am now giving a reference letter and credibility to the sales truths you will read in this book.

My life has changed for the better since that time of nervous unknown in August of 2003. I have become a student of sales and learned the secret to success is to control one's thinking. I have studied Earl Nightingale, Jeffrey Gitomer, and Brian Tracy. I have flooded my mind with speeches of Mort Utley, Vince Lombardi, and Dr. Norman Vincent Peal. I read daily in books such as *The 8th Habit*, *How to Win Friends and Influence People*, and the *Holy Bible*. The one common denominator is that you truly do become what you think about. You are going to get exactly what you put into this life. Learning sales under David Otis has been no different than what any of these great authors have proclaimed.

David has a passion for helping others get what they want out of life. I have been a part of that first hand. I wanted bigger and better things for my future, and David told me that if I would follow some simple guidelines, that I could certainly attain them. They are all found in this book. They are not hard to follow, and the simplicity of them is mysterious in itself. That is why not everyone who is introduced to these simple principles will fully believe them when they read this book. The one thing that no one can do for you is to believe in your abilities and your determination to achieve your goals and will them to happen. That is up to you. I am here to say that if you want great things to become a reality and you want to reach a higher level of achievement or help lead others to higher levels of achievement—you can! The great thing about it is you do not have to invent the roadmap to success. The formula is contained in this book, and you just have to provide the vehicle to take you there.

Passion and desire is not something you can teach. It has to come from within you. Neither I, nor David, or anyone else mentioned in this book can do that for you. However, you hold in your hands a great system and method for success. It has worked for me and continues to work for me as a sales leader to change the future of my sales representatives as well.

Don't let another day go by filled with mediocrity. Life can get away from you fast. Take the desire and passion that is within you and apply these simple truths to it. Become a student of sales. Create a mindset of the positive and never lean towards the negative. Digest this system and instill the habits it takes to achieve and YOU WILL ACHIEVE.

David, I want to thank you for sticking with me and never giving me a negative thought and never giving up on me. You were right when you said, "I can't do it for you but if you will just apply this system and your desire for great things YOU WILL GET THEM." David, I am getting them like I never thought possible, and they continue to come. My life is better at work and at home. Thank you for creating an environment instead of reacting to one when you assumed the sales leadership role in that tiny broken down branch in Chattanooga, Tennessee. Those will forever be, "The good ole days."

Jeremy Wood

ABOUT THE AUTHOR

David Otis was one of the top sales representatives for a Fortune 500 company for eight years and a top sales leader for the past three years. David is currently the sales manager for the Chattanooga, Tennessee market. Prior to David's arrival to the Chattanooga market three years ago, the market was one of the poorest performing markets in the company. By applying basic sales skills and a change of attitude, the Chattanooga market is now one of the top five performing markets in the company out of 350 locations nationwide.

David speaks at meetings throughout his company and with other organizations. His passion and enthusiasm create energizing and engaging presentations. If you hear David's presentation you will never forget it!

Your organization can benefit from David's 17 years of sales and leadership experience. It is a simple approach that the leadership and sales representatives alike will love. It is truly sales made easy.

This Book Is Dedicated To Dick Surdykowski, Dave Prebenda, And Mark Biasucci.

I Would Like To Thank You For The Opportunity To Work For Such A Great Company.
March 15, 1995, You Made A Decision That Changed The Direction Of My Life For The Better. You Hired Me.
I Had Just Turned Thirty Years Of Age. I Was Single And Dead Broke. If You Remember I Wrote You A $200 Check My First Week On The Job To Attend A Seminar And That Check Bounced!
Nearly Ten Short Years Later I Have A Home On The 18th Hole Of A Private Golf Course; And Not Only Support Myself In Finer Fashion Than I Could Have Ever Dreamed, I Also Support My Lovely Wife, Laura, And Our Two Beautiful Children, Billy And Jamie Ann.
I Have Benefited From The Application Of A Great Corporate Culture. You Hired Partners Who Fit Our Culture, Provided Training, And Placed Us In A Positive Environment, Which Allowed Partners Like Me To Reach Our Full Potential. For That I Thank You.

INTRODUCTION

I grew up on a farm in Kentucky. My father was a basketball coach, school bus driver, high school basketball referee, schoolteacher, and a full time farmer. My mother was a schoolteacher and a full time homemaker. When they had time to relax or sleep, I do not know. They provided my two brothers and me the best childhood I could imagine.

I knew I did not want to be a farmer. The first time I saw my dad castrate a young calf I was certain I would never make it as a farmer.

In my last semester of college at the University of Kentucky I did an internship at a local television station in the sales department. Sales looked like a lot more fun than farming, so I decided that would be my future.

After graduation, I took the five hundred dollars my grandparents gave me and set out for California. I knew there had to be more to life than what I had experienced growing up in rural Kentucky, so I decided to go see how the rest of the world was living.

I checked into a motel after forty-eight hours of driving across the country. The next day I went in pursuit of a sales job. I started with an advertising agency referred by the sales manager at the television station in Kentucky. After my interview, the agency informed me that my experience did not warrant a sales position but they were in need of a sales assistant. They asked my earning expectations, and without hesitation, I informed them that I needed to make 1,000 dollars per month. Of course they hired me. Little did I know that in Los Angeles rent was more than 1,000 per month! Somehow I found a place to live and survived one year in L.A. before deciding to pursue my destiny in Atlanta, Georgia.

Once in Atlanta I decided it was time for me to get some real sales experience so I called my older brother John, who was doing quite well selling insurance, and asked him to help me get a job with his company in Georgia. One week later I was in a sales training class in Dallas, Texas. I was now officially a sales representative, but not a very good one I might add.

I assumed because my brother sold for this company and did well that I would also do well. What I failed to realize is that in sales you are paid for results, not for efforts.

This was a 100% commission sales job. No benefits and no expense accounts. We paid our own expenses from hotel rooms, meals, to marketing. We sold supplemental insurance to school teachers. My first few weeks after training I had failed to make a sale. Three straight zero weeks. I was going nowhere fast. In desperation I went to the bookstore and found a book on sales. I did it so I could at least look busy in the teacher's lounge, because I sure wasn't selling anything. Then something amazing happened. I started getting into a positive frame of mind while reading. I also picked up some sales tips.

I will never forget! It was at the end of my first month with this company, it was Friday afternoon, I hadn't sold anything, and I was finally out of money. I was near tears when four teachers approached me in the library at Burk Elementary School in Savannah, Georgia. I think God sent them to me, because they said they wanted to buy my insurance. I said with all the confidence I could muster, "Are you sure?" $613.87 was my commission. I sold the applications to my sales manager Bill Smith and had enough money to stay in sales for another week. Sixteen years later I am still surviving.

YOU ARE IN SALES

This book was written for the person with the desire to go from an ordinary sales person to a professional sales person. The ordinary sales person believes circumstances control their destiny. They blame their lack of success on everything and everyone except themselves. They typically change jobs every two to three years in search of the perfect sales job. The professional sales person accepts responsibility for everything that happens in their life. Their results consistently rank in the top ten percent. They receive the recognition and the big commission checks.

No matter what it says on your business card, and even if you do not have a business card, you are in sales. The only questions are do you realize it, and are you good at it? If you have children, you are in sales. If you are a plant manager, you are in sales. If you are a secretary, you are in sales. If you are a human resource manager, you are in sales. No matter what your business card says, you are in sales.

My hope is that the principles contained in this book will help you not only become better at the art of persuasion, but in the art of communication.

"Help enough people get what they want and you will get what you want."
Zig Ziglar

Example:

A human resource manager recently requested to join the sales department stating that he thought he would make an excellent sales person. After reviewing his performance it was discovered his 401K enrollment was around sixty percent. This was a major responsibility of the human resource manager. The problem was he was not doing a very good job selling the employees on enrolling in the plan. He was in sales already and did not realize it. After this was brought to his attention he decided to become a better sales person.

He developed a plan to find his prospects, and get an appointment with them to sell the 401K. He developed good business related questions and a presentation of the 401K plan. He showed the partners how much participating in the plan would benefit them at retirement. He then asked them to enroll in the plan (closed) and handled their objections.

Just like that the enrollment increased by twenty-five percent! No matter what, you are in sales! Now get good!

CHAPTER ONE
ACRE OF DIAMONDS

D r. Russell Herman Conwell, the founder of Temple
University, told a story during his speaking tour
raising money to form this university. I would like to
share it with you as told by Earl Nightingale.

*In 1840, there was a farmer who settled in Africa. He
settled there because he had heard the exciting stories of
other African settlers who had discovered diamonds and
made millions. This was not unusual because Africa was
rich in diamonds.*

*He could hardly wait to sell his farm and search for
diamonds. He spent the rest of his life searching the vast
African continent for the shinning gems that would make
him rich but without success. Finally, in a fit of despair,
broke and despondent, he threw himself into a river and
drowned.*

*Meanwhile, the man who had bought his farm, one day
while walking around the property, found a large and
unusual stone. The stone turned out to be a diamond of
enormous value. The property was covered with diamonds.
It was to become one of the world's richest diamond mines.
Now the first farmer had owned literally acres of diamonds,
but sold it for nearly nothing, in order to go search for*

diamonds elsewhere. If he had only taken the time to know what diamonds look like in their rough state and first searched the property that he currently owned, he would have had the millions he desired.

Ladies and Gentlemen, we are sitting on an acre of diamonds. There is no need to go in search of greener pastures. The riches you desire are more readily available than at any other time in the history of the world. The change you need is most likely not a change of jobs but a change in attitude and skill. My intent in the pages that follow is to help you learn how to mine these diamonds.

Have you ever heard someone say that the other top sales reps in their company are just lucky? Some of the best sales reps I have known made it look easy, and most of them have been with the same company a long time and have worked hard to perfect their trade. Is this just coincidence, or is there something to be learned here?

I remember my first experience in sales. I was twenty-three years old selling insurance to schoolteachers. Our sales manager would assign the sales reps schools to work for the week. We had one gentleman, Howard Thrower, who always seemed to get the "good" schools. That was the only explanation I could come up with to explain why Howard would sell so much more than I would. What I did not realize at the time was Howard sold more than me because he was more professional and skilled than I was. If I raised my professionalism and skill level, my results would improve. I would start to get "good" schools too! The problem with most average or struggling sales reps is that they think they are pretty good sales people. They believe that others cause their struggles. They think it is because of their company, their boss, their territory, their products, their pricing, the competition. They have all sorts of excuses they believe are holding them back from becoming top performers. What they fail to realize is the real problem is them. The problem usually goes back to a lack of professionalism and sales skill.

I will give you a real life example. When I arrived in Chattanooga, Tennessee three years ago to lead the worst sales team in the company, we had a sales rep that was one of the worst in our group. My first assignment was to get him to improve his results or fire him. I met Tate at eight in the morning to start our first day together. I asked Tate how he liked his job, and he said it was great. I asked him what he liked about sales and he said, "I love the freedom and riding around meeting people." I then asked Tate to assess his performance after one year in sales with the company. He said he thought he was doing a pretty good job. I asked him to assess his skill level as a sales rep, and Tate said he was a great sales person. He believed he was maybe the best on the team. He said he would prove it if I gave him a new territory.

Sound familiar? So we leave the office to start the day in the field. The first appointment was at nine o'clock. The appointment was with an undesirable prospect, and the person we were meeting did not even make the decision for our service. Tate began by immediately stating that he could help the prospect keep his building clean, dry, and safe while at the same time reducing depreciation on their carpet. The business was a boat marina and they had a large dog chewing at the ragged edges of their carpet. Tate forged ahead assuming incorrectly the prospects buying motives and once again stating that he had a solution for the prospects business. The prospect once again informed Tate that they did not care about their carpet. He said, "We are a marina, and besides the dog will chew up the carpet anyway." Tate continued until we were finally asked to leave. Tate said proudly to me as we got back in the car, "You see, I don't take no for an answer. Prospects will have to kick me out to get me to stop asking for the business." Tate thought he was really good.

Our next appointment was a very small business that did not meet our requirements to provide our service. The owner quickly stated, "I am closing the business within the next few months." Tate ignored this information and continued to get started on his less than stellar presentation of products and services. No rapport building or asking questions, he just jumped into his products and services. At this point I had seen enough and cut the presentation short. Tate and I excused ourselves and ended the prospect's misery. Tate was furious. He was certain his new boss had cost him a sale.

I told Tate to drive to the nearest bookstore. He thought I knew something about selling our products and services to bookstores so he quickly headed to a bookstore. We walked in, and I took him to the business section. I picked out one of my favorite books on sales, and we headed for the counter. Tate was waiting for me to pay the cashier. When Tate realized the book was for him, and he had to pay for it, he was furious again. We got outside and Tate said, "You sure know how to pick expensive books!" I replied, "Tate if I told you to put $30 in an account and in two years it will be worth $10,000, would you do it?" Tate said, "Of course I would." I informed Tate that is exactly what you have just done except it will be worth a lot more than $10,000 if you read, practice, and apply the basic sales principles talked about in the book.

To make a long story short Tate is now an avid student of sales and has become a top performer. He has doubled his income, and we laugh about the days when he thought he was good. By the way Tate's territory did not change, pricing did not change, his boss is still a jerk, and he works for the same company. The only change Tate made was in his skill and his attitude. **Try it! It works!**

Everyone loves to arrive, but few love to travel. To arrive in sales and in life you have to endure the difficult times, and not only endure them but learn to enjoy them. The difficult times are the period when true character is built. These are the times that make you appreciate the good times. The most worthwhile things don't come easy. If a sales career was easy, then everyone would do it, and it would not pay very well. This is why it is so important to get with a good company and stay with them a long time. Your first two or three years in sales and in a territory are the toughest. The first year should be the hardest you ever work and the least money you ever made. Don't make the mistake that many people do. They work their first two or three years for their entire career. By that I mean they change jobs every two or three years. Sometimes change is necessary but most often the change we need is within ourselves. We need to change our habits and our approach.

CHAPTER TWO
HABITS

*I am your constant companion. I am your greatest helper
or heaviest burden. I will push you onward or drag you
down to failure. I am completely at your command. Half
the things you do you might just as well turn over to me,
and I will be able to do them quickly and correctly.*

*I am easily managed; you must merely be firm with me.
Show me exactly how you want something done, and after
a few lessons, I will do it automatically. I am the servant
of all great people; and alas, of all failures as well. Those
who are great, I have made great. Those who are failures,
I have made fail.*

*I am not a machine, though I work with all the precision
of a machine, plus the intelligence of a human being. You
may run me for profit or turn me for ruin; it makes no
difference to me.*

*Take me, train me, be firm with me, and I will place the
world at your feet. Be easy with me and I will destroy
you.*

Who am I? I AM A HABIT

-Anonymous

A good habit is not easily formed but once it is formed,
it will change your results forever. Experts say it takes twenty-

one days to form a habit. Ask yourself, "Do I want my desired result enough to spend twenty-one days forming habits that will come to you automatically."

- Good habits = good results
- Bad habits = bad results
- Inconsistent habits = inconsistent results

And on and on it goes. So if you want great results in sales and in life, you need to form great habits.

What are great sales habits?

- Exercise your mind and body thirty minutes each day.
- Start each day with thirty minutes of positive reading. Examples are the *Holy Bible*, Jeffery Gitomer's *Sales Bible*, or Napoleon Hill's *Think and Grow Rich*. Brian Tracy, Zig Ziglar and Ken Blanchard have several great books to choose from. Go to Amazon.com or booksurge.com to see what is available.

Get in the habit of appreciating how lucky we are to be born in the land of opportunity. The odds of being born in America at this time in history to a half—way decent family are less than buying a winning lottery ticket. We are one of the only generations in the history of the world that has luxuries such at cable television, radios, CD Players, light bulbs, and indoor plumbing.

My mother had to go to an outhouse to use the restroom when she was a child. Prior generations spent most, if not all, of their money on necessities. We spend most of our money on luxuries. There are people living in third world countries that will never have the opportunities that you and I have. Yet we find ourselves complaining. The problem is not that we have it too difficult. The problem is we have it too easy.

One day a man saw a butterfly, shuddering on the sidewalk, locked in a seemingly hopeless struggle to free itself from its now useless cocoon. Feeling pity, he took a pocketknife, carefully cut away the cocoon and set the butterfly free. To his dismay, it lay on the sidewalk, convulsed weakly for a while, and died. A biologist later told him, "That was the worst thing you could have done! A butterfly needs that struggle to develop the muscles to fly. By robbing him of the struggle, you made him too weak to live."
Author unknown

We have been robbed of the struggle. Let's stop complaining! Remember when times get difficult, and they will, you are developing strength. This strength will be an asset to you down the road to help others overcome their struggles. As Winston Churchill said, "If you are going through Hell, keep going!" All things will come to pass. The good times will not last and the bad times won't either. Get in the habit of telling your family how much you love and appreciate them. Get in the habit of seeing the positive side of every situation. Remember that positive thoughts will produce positive results. Get in the habit of giving 100% of yourself to your profession, remembering that a successful career is just a series of successful days. So make each day a successful day.

Get in the habit of setting goals. Establish long-term goals (where you want to be in ten years) and short-term goals (what you want to achieve this month or quarter), and then set a game plan to achieve these goals.

When establishing goals start with the end in mind. You must first decide what you want to accomplish with your life and career. This may require some thought. You can not just "drift" through life and hope to wind up at the destination you desire. You must create a road map for success. Things are first created in your mind, and then you can make them reality. Aim high when setting your goals. Stretch yourself but make them attainable. Remember your short-term goals should ultimately help you achieve our long-term goals. Once your goals are set, start living them now. For example, dress for the job you want not the job you have. You are capable of far more than you realize.

Be sure to write your goals down and review your progress several times each year. Find areas where you could have done better and adjust your plan if you need to.

Most people take their commitments seriously. Make a commitment to yourself and hold yourself accountable. Remember, winning is fun, and it pays well, so guarantee yourself success. When you face challenges, and you will, stay positive and persist. Never give up! See yourself having already attained the status you desire and just think how inspiring your story will be to others when you overcome your challenges. If it was easy, anyone could do it, and it wouldn't pay very well.

GOAL PLANNING WORKSHEET

My mission statement in life is:

My job title in five years will be:

My job title in ten years will be:

My sales goal this year is:

I will achieve the following awards this year:

I will do the following to improve myself this year: (read what books, attend what seminars, exercise)

What does my house look like in ten years? What kind of car will I drive?

How much money will I have in my savings account in 10 years:

How my friends will describe me in five years:

GAME PLAN TO CREATE THE LIFE I DESIRE

Weekly Routine:
Monday:

Tuesday:

Wednesday:

Thursday:

Friday:

Saturday:

Sunday:

Remember that your success in your career will be largely dependent on the quality of your game plan. You can't depend on just luck.

Earl Nightingale says in his recording, *"The Strangest Secret"* that, "We become what we think about." So place your goals and game plan in a visible place so you can see them every day. Remember, a successful life and career is just a series of successful days so go have seven great days!

You have to have a system or method that you can count on for positive results. Establish a good routine and stick to it. Remember the first month will require effort; after that it will come to you automatically.

Napoleon Hill would call your long-term goal your "purpose." He studied 500 of the most successful people in America during the early 1900's and noticed that they had similar traits and habits that led them to achieve unprecedented success in various fields during a difficult time in this country's history.

The starting point of all achievement, according to Napoleon Hill, is a **BURNING DESIRE TO WIN.** He tells a story in his book *Think and Grow Rich* to illustrate this point.

There was a great warrior who led his army into battle. They faced a formidable opponent whose army outnumbered their own. They loaded their boats with soldiers and equipment, sailed to the enemy's country, unloaded the boats and equipment. The warrior then gave the order to set the boats on fire. With the smoke rising from the boats the warrior told his men, "You see the boats going up in smoke.

That means we cannot leave these shores alive. **We win or**
we perish.*" They won.*

This is a true story. It is a story of William the Conqueror
in 1066 when the Normans invaded England. This was the last
time anyone has successfully invaded England.

People generally get what they want. The question you
have to ask yourself now that you have established you goals
is, "Do I want to achieve this goal bad enough to persist when
times get difficult?" If you have established a worthwhile goal,
you will be tested.

It has been said that the life of a sales person is a roller
coaster ride. You will experience the highs of all highs and the
lows of all lows. Here is a poem I kept in my pocket and read
almost daily my first year in sales. It gave me hope during the
difficult times. I hope it does the same for you.

Don't Quit

When things go wrong, as they sometimes will,
When the road you're trudging seems all uphill,
When the funds are low and the debts are high,
And you want to smile, but you have to sigh,
When care is pressing you down a bit,
Rest, if you must, but do not quit.
Life is queer with its twists and turns,
As every one of us sometimes learns,
And many a failure turns about,
When he might have won had he stuck it out;
Don't give up, though the pace seems slow—
You may succeed with another blow.

Often the goal is nearer than
It seems to faint and faltering man,
Often the struggler has given up,
When he might have captured the victor's cup,
And he learned too late when the night slipped down,
How close he was to the golden crown.
Success is failure turned inside out—
The silver tint of the clouds of doubt,
And you never can tell how close you are,
It may be near when it seems so far,
So stick to the fight when you're hardest hit—
It's when things seem worst that you must not quit.
Anonymous

Many times people quit, or give themselves a back-up plan in case it does not work out in their current career or position. This mindset rarely produces GREATNESS. To achieve greatness retreat cannot be an option. Failure must be seen as just a temporary set back. It must be, "**We win or perish!**"

CHAPTER THREE
A CALL TO GREATNESS

This is a call to everyone that reads this and cares enough to answer. This is a call to greatness.

What is greatness? I have put some thought into this matter and have come to the conclusion: **greatness is the pursuit of excellence.** You do not have to be a professional athlete, a president, or famous to achieve greatness.

My grandfather was a plumber and my father believes his dad was a great man. I have to agree. Claude Otis was in pursuit of excellence. My father tells a story that demonstrates Claude's pursuit.

Claude was known to carry a level with him at all times. He would constantly inspect his work to make sure everything was plumb. One day he put his level up to a pipe and noticed it was ever so slightly off. Claude ordered his fellow plumber to tear the work down and redo it so that it was perfect. His fellow plumber protested, "It is close enough!" It will work fine, and besides we are putting a wall over the pipes. The customer will never know the difference!" Claude replied, "They won't know, but you will know, and I will know. Tear it down and make it plumb!"

To Claude Otis it was bigger than plumbing. He was in pursuit of excellence. It was about doing the right thing, because it was the right thing to do. As a result, Claude gained a reputation as being a great plumber. He was in demand while other plumbers struggled to get work. Customers were willing to hire Claude without even asking his price! They knew they could trust him to deliver superior quality at a fair price.

My grandfather did not pursue money. He pursued excellence, and as a by-product he became rich in character, and never wanted for money. He lived a rich full life, and passed on priceless values to my father who passed them on to his children. He answered the call. Will you?

STEPS TO ACHIEVEMENT
1) DECIDE WHAT YOU WANT.
    A) To achieve anything worthwhile you must first decide what you want.
    B) You must have a "BURNING DESIRE" to achieve this goal.
2) COMMIT TO YOUR DECIDED POSITION AND COMPANY.
    This is important because if you have set a worthwhile, goal you will be challenged and may even be tempted to give up.

Persistence is the enemy of mediocrity!
3) ATTAIN THE SKILL NEEDED TO PERFORM AT A HIGH LEVEL.
4) ESTABLISH A ROUTINE AND STICK TO IT!
    Remember a successful career is just a series of successful days. So go have seven great days this week!

I have heard it said that there are two ways to get rich.

One is to get with a good company and stay with them a long time. The other is to start your own business. When I use the word rich I am not only referring to money. Some of the poorest people I have ever known have led rich full lives, and some of the richest people I have ever known have led empty lives. What I am talking about is a rich full life. Money many times will be a by-product of living a rich full life.

For example: When you were single you had the choice of hundreds of partners to marry (If you are currently single you still have this choice). Now you could stay with this partner for a few years and when times get difficult, and they will, you can leave that partner and find another partner. You can stay with that partner for a few years and when times get difficult, and they will, you can again leave. Will this lead to a rich full successful life? Maybe, however it is not likely. It is the same with a career. Find a good company and make a commitment.

Determination and persistence will produce great results when mixed with a **BURNING DESIRE TO WIN**. Be creative and look for new and better ways to do your job. Avoid people who say, "Can't." Challenge yourself to get a little better each day, and refuse to let anything stand in your way.

Earl Nightingale has a CD that I recommend every person have in his or her library called *"The Strangest Secret"*. He says the secret of success is **"You become what you think about."** If you want to be a top performer you must think like a top performer. To do this you need to know what top performers think about. Get to know the best sales people in your company and associate with winners. Avoid negative people at all cost!

INTERVIEW WITH A WINNER:

This is an interview of my teammate Terri Norris from Jeffery Gitomer's column published July 27th 2001.

Terri's Top 10:

Here, in her own words, are the Top Ten qualities and characteristics of what makes Terri Norris No 1:

1) **A contagious positive attitude:** *I believe that I am blessed and that positive things will happen in my life. Because I believe that positive things will happen to me, they do!*

2) **Excited about the prospect of helping others.** *Sincerely caring. When I have appointments, I want to help my prospective customers solve a problem, get better service, increase productivity, etc. I believe that they can sense that I want to help them and not "sell them something".*

3) **Self assured, not arrogant.** *Confidence. I know that I can achieve whatever I decide to and am willing to work hard for. I believe in my abilities and myself.*

4) **I like people and they like me.** *People like me right away. I'm not a threat to them. And I'm not perceived as "salesy". Being able to relate to people, all people. I don't try to "typecast" people; I just try to "like" them.*

5) **Not just book smart.** *Being able to assess and solve real-world problems. Being able to prioritize and decide which things (prospects) to spend time on and which ones not to. Work smarter, not harder.*

6) *If I'm not having fun, what's the point?* *I have often been described as easily amused. I think this is one of my best characteristics. I find joy in almost everything.*

7) *I do everything full force. I sweat when I work and I sweat when I dance. The minimum acceptable standard is 110%. If something is worthwhile, I give it everything I have.*

8) *Unspoken integrity. Visibly honest. I try to be honest and ethical in everything I do. I feel that being trustworthy and honorable is a strong statement of character. I try to always keep my promises. Hopefully, my word means something to others, because it means everything to me.*

9) *I concentrate on the details without getting caught up in them. Beyond organized. Detail is vital to my success. It sounds minute, but it is huge. I keep things in order so I can function error-free. I try not to waste time or energy by trying to find things twice or picking up dropped balls.*

10) *I'm kid-like happy on the inside. I have the enthusiasm of a two—year-old with a college degree and a business card. I am the eternal cheerleader for others and myself. I want everyone to win (except my competition).*

TO BE A WINNER JUST THINK AND ACT LIKE A WINNER!

Remember how your parents warned you to pick your friends carefully because you will become like those you associate with? The same holds true throughout life. Positive thoughts and positive actions always produce positive results over time. Unfortunately, the reverse holds true, negative thoughts will produce negative results. It sounds too simple to believe that by controlling your thoughts you can control your results. It is simple. However, it is not easy to control your thinking. It takes practice and effort.

Here is an exercise that if done will change your life forever: Get up every morning and read thirty minutes in a positive book such as Napoleon Hill's *Think and Grow Rich,* or Jeffery Gitomer's *The Sales Bible.* Brian Tracy has several books and CD's that you should read and listen to. This will train your mind to think in a positive manner as well as give you new creative ideas. By reading thirty minutes a day you will become an expert in five years. Experts make great money. Sales is the world's highest paid profession, if you are good at it. Unfortunately, sales is also the world's lowest paid profession if you are not. So get good!

Everyone wants to be successful, but not everyone is willing to do what is necessary to become successful. It amazes me how many people never study their business. Would you see a doctor who did not study in his field of practice? Would you see a lawyer who never studied law? The best doctors and lawyers studied for years, and continue their education to become the best in their profession. If you want to become the very best in your field you must do the same. You need to view yourself as a professional. Simply become a student of sales and leadership, and learn to control the way you think.

CHAPTER FOUR
BECOME A PROFESSIONAL SALES PERSON

The best friends of success are faith, hope, enthusiasm, and belief. The enemies of success are fear and doubt. It is natural for fear and doubt to creep into our thoughts from time to time. The key to overcoming fear and doubt is to realize it is there, and have a method to get back into a positive frame of mind. Have you ever wondered what successful people think about most of the time? They think about what they want and how they are going to get it. Average people think about their bills, problems, or wonder if they can hit their quota and keep their jobs. Remember, to be a top performer, all you have to do is think and act like a top performer. The key word is act. For example, to become enthusiastic you must first act enthusiastic!

A great way to fake enthusiasm is to **WALK FAST! TALK LOUD! AND SMILE!** If I told you my wife just left me and took off with my best friend, but I said it talking loud and smiling, you would think I was happy about it. Get the picture? People love to buy from people who enjoy what they do. Act enthusiastic and you will become enthusiastic. **Your aim should be to become the most positive, enthusiastic person you know!**

A person can succeed at almost anything for which he or she has unlimited enthusiasm.
Charles M. Schwab

I was recently visiting my 91-year-old grandfather and noticed a book on the shelf that was my grandmother's. It was a book by the late Dr. Norman Vincent Peale. I began to read a story about enthusiasm. This is a real life example of how acting enthusiastic can work in your favor.

A baseball player by the name of Frank Bettger was playing in what today would be the equivalent of the Triple A league and making $175 per month. This was good money in 1907. One day the manager called Frank into his office and fired him. Frank was shocked and asked a question that altered the course of his life. He asked the manager, "why?" The answer shocked him even more. The manager informed him that he was fired because he was lazy. He told Frank that he ran around the bases like a veteran who had played for 20 years. He said, "Frank what ever you do after you leave here, for heaven's sake, wake yourself up, and put some life and enthusiasm into your work!"
After being fired Frank went down to a lower league and began playing for a team at $25 per month. Hardly anything to be excited about. However he took the manager's advice and began to act enthusiastic. According to the story he made up his mind to establish a reputation of being the most enthusiastic ballplayer they'd ever seen in the New

England League. He thought if he could establish such a reputation, then he'd have to live up to it.

From the minute he stepped onto the field he acted like a man electrified. As he threw the baseball around the infield he almost knocked the other player's gloves off. Once, apparently trapped, he slid into third base with so much energy and force that the third baseman fumbled the ball and Frank was able to score an important run. Yes, it was all a show, an act he was putting on. Did it work? It worked like magic! Frank's enthusiasm sparked his teammates, and they began to become excited. Soon he was back in the Triple A league. And two years later Frank Bettger was playing for the St. Louis Cardinals and had increased his income 700 times. What did it? Enthusiasm alone did it, nothing but enthusiasm.

It worked for Frank Bettger playing baseball back in 1907, and it will work for you today in sales. Try it!

The first task is to decide what you want. You must then focus your thoughts and energy toward obtaining your goal. Associate with like-minded individuals, and let nothing stand in your way. **Accept responsibility for everything that happens in your life.** Accepting responsibility earns the respect of your superiors, peers, and subordinates alike. Accepting responsibility gives you power and control over your life. If you say, "It is not my fault," and make excuses, then you lose control. What you are saying is, "I am a victim," "I am helpless." When you accept responsibility, you take control and can make positive change.

Our lives are not shaped by what happens to us, but with how we deal with what happens to us. There are few things in life that we can control; however, the one thing we can control is the one thing that matters most and will have the biggest impact on our success or failure. **We can control our thinking!** Remember your thoughts will become your actions; your actions will become your results. If you want to control your results you must control your thoughts and direct them on the desired result. Simple, right? Simple but not easy, this takes practice and focus.

MAKE A GREAT FIRST IMPRESSION:

It is important to make a great impression. A prospect will form a lasting impression of you in the first thirty to sixty seconds. **Dress for success!**

Your physical appearance is the first thing people will notice about you. Fair or not, you will be judged on your appearance and this will have a lasting impression on everyone you meet. Some things about our appearance we cannot change. The important things we can.

- SHINE YOUR SHOES DAILY
- PRESS YOUR SHIRTS
- KEEP YOUR HAIR NEAT AND PROFESSIONAL
- NO EXCESS COLOGNE OR PERFUME
- WALK FAST
- TALK LOUD AND SMILE!

Look at the most highly paid successful executives and notice the detail they put into their dress. How you dress tells people about you, the good and the bad. Be aware of your first impression and strive to improve it.

SEPARATE WORK AND PERSONAL MATTERS:

When you are at work focus on work, and when you are at home focus on your home life. I have seen many sales reps take personal calls during the workday. Do yourself a favor and limit these calls. I would recommend returning personal calls at noon if absolutely necessary and 4:45pm if possible.

Keep your mind focused on your work goals during the workday. This may sound unreasonable at first glance but consider this: If you do not separate your work and personal life, the two will begin to interfere with one another and you will not be great at either.

If you take personal calls during the sales day you may lose focus on your work. This can cause your performance to be below expectations, which will cause stress at home. In turn you will begin to talk about your work problems at home. How your boss is an unreasonable jerk and your territory stinks. You will begin to talk and think about your personal life at work; how the bills are accumulating. Get the picture? The invention of the cell phone was great for sales people; however, it also can allow the mixing of business and personal lives during the workday. STOP IT AND FOCUS ON WORK AT WORK AND HOME AT HOME!

MANAGE YOUR TIME WELL:

One thing everyone has in common is the number of hours in each day. Many times the only difference between the top sales people and the average sales person is how they choose to use their time. A great rule you can apply to your day is the 80/20 Rule, also known as Pareto's Principle. In 1906, Italian economist Vilfredo Pareto, created a mathematical formula to describe the unequal distribution of wealth in France. He observed that 20 percent of the people owned 80 percent of the wealth. He called this 20 percent the "vital few." The other 80 percent of the population he called the "trivial many." You can use this law to manage your time. Spend 80 percent of your time doing the "vital few" activities that will lead to a sale. These include prospecting, presenting, and closing. Spend 20 percent of your time on the "trivial many" activities that are necessary such as paperwork. This helps you manage those things that really make a difference to your results. In sales, results obtained the right way are all that matter.

Don't confuse activity with achievement.
John Wooden

One great way to be more efficient in your territory is to divide your territory into three or four smaller territories. Set appointments in each territory for the same day. Try to be in these smaller territories the same day each week. Stick to it, and only vary from your schedule when absolutely necessary. This will reduce the amount of time you spend driving around. You will need to get out of the car to make a sale!

PROSPECTING:

In order to make a sale you will need a prospect. Your company may have a prospect base established already. If they do that is wonderful. If they do not it is no big deal. Remember that you are responsible. There are many places to find prospects. Order a manufactures guide from each state in your territory. This will give you every business in your state, the address, the contacts and titles.

Go to the Chamber of Commerce in each city and purchase a list of members and area businesses. They will also give you a copy of the phone book. Yellow Pages are a great source for prospects because they have purchased advertising. Go online and look under Yellowpages.com. Be prepared and have a game plan before you sit down and make phone calls for appointments. Know what area and what businesses you wish to contact. This will make your time more effective. Remember that time is what you exchange for money.

Join the area Chamber of Commerce and go to events so you can get to know the business leaders in your territory. Join a networking group. Ask every appointment if they know of anyone who can use your products or services. Look for ways to work smarter, not harder.

DEVELOP A SEED LETTER CAMPAIGN:

The idea is to get the prospects to call you or be waiting on your call. Be creative, and make your mailer memorable. Your mailer campaign should be done on a targeted number of prospects on a regular schedule. A good way to do this is to target fifty accounts and send them a seed mailer once each quarter.

WAYS TO MAKE YOUR MAILERS MEMORABLE:

Idea #1) Put a few lollipops in an envelope along with a letter that says in bold print, "TIRED OF BEING A SUCKER FOR POOR SERVICE AND PRICE INCREASES! Then give me a call and see why customers like XYZ Company, and ABC Company trust us to deliver superior quality at a fair price."

Idea #2) Mail a fishing lure in an envelope along with a letter that says in bold print, "CATCH A GREAT DEAL! See why companies who want world class products and service such as XYZ Company and ABC Company chose us."

Idea #3) Send a fax to the prospect offering a free golf shirt for all that grant an appointment. Include a form the prospect can fill out and fax back to cash in on the offer. Be sure to include the names of current customers who are in a similar industry as your prospect.

Idea #4) Send videotaped testimonials of your current customers to your prospect along with some popcorn. Have a catchy cover letter that will entice the prospect to watch the video.

INTRODUCING YOURSELF TO THE PROSPECT:

Now that you have identified you prospects you will need a great introductory statement that you use to get an appointment. Some people call this an opening statement. According to Jeffrey Gitomer, make your introduction a **POWER STATEMENT.**

To develop an introduction of your company and yourself, remember to make your statement short and to the point using the names of current customers that your prospect will recognize. When you deliver your statement, talk loud with a smile. A basic rule in sales and life is the Golden Rule, *"Treat others how you want to be treated."* Imagine yourself as the prospect and ask what would make me respond in a positive manner? You could even use what has been referred to as the Platinum Rule, *"Treat others the way they want to be treated."* This rule requires more skill.

The purpose of your introduction is to enable you to make appointments either by phone or on a cold call in the field. Remember, the better your introduction, the more appointments you will have.

When cold calling or setting appointments by phone, remember the objective is to get the appointment. The more you talk the less likely you are to get the appointment. Do not make the mistake of asking, "I see you have a _____, are you happy with it?" Give your introduction statement and ask for the appointment! If they say, "we are happy," you can reply, "Great, well I just want to be your backup in case something changes down the road, and I am going to be out here tomorrow at 8 am. Will 8 am be ok?"

Continue to improve your introduction and practice in front of your fellow sales reps or family members and ask them what they think. A good way to evaluate the quality of your introduction is to imagine yourself at your twenty-year high school reunion and a former classmate asks, "What do you do for a living?"

After hearing your statement your classmate thinks, "Wow, I wish I worked for a great company like that," or "Poor Joe, I really thought he might make something of himself." Get the picture?

Example of an Opening Statement:

Good morning! My name is David Otis with XYZ Corporation. We help companies such as ABC Company, KLM Company, as well as Joe's Company next door increase their customer retention and make more money through increasing employee morale. I would like to come by Monday at 9 A.M. and show you how we can do the same for your business. Will that be OK?

PREPARE YOURSELF:

Be organized and use a day timer to log your appointments. Be sure to include complete information in your day timer. Full company name, address with zip code, phone number, and email address. Remember you are a professional. This day timer can be used in the future as a reference. You can look back and see what your successful weeks looked like and what your not so successful weeks looked like also. Discover what works and repeat it!

Now that you have the appointment, get ready. The amount of preparation you do for an account depends on the product you are selling and the size of the account. However, you never want to call on a prospect unprepared. Professional sales people know their business. They are experts and are seen as consultants rather than salespeople.

It is easier to prepare for a sales call today than it has ever been in the history of sales. All the information you ever wanted to know about your prospect can most likely be found on the Internet. Visit their facility and look around. You are looking for ways you can help the prospect improve their current way of doing business. When you find a way to help the prospect you will be more enthusiastic about setting the appointment.

Create a pre-call planning worksheet. To be seen as an expert you must act like one. Plan your call and prepare for possible objections and address them upfront. Do not ignore possible objections to your product or services. Be pro-active and address them and provide solutions.

EXAMPLE PRE-CALL PLANNING WORKSHEET:

Date of appointment
Company name
Address
Phone number
Decision-maker
Others involved in decision process
Set the agenda for the appointment

Rapport building questions

Possible buying motive

Present Company with National and Local references (list at least 5)

Products and services which may interest the prospect

What are the benefits of the products and services to the prospect

Potential objections

Plan to overcome objections

Now that you have prepared yourself, you are ready to make the presentation. When you arrive for your appointment, be on time. When you arrive late it shows that you do not value their time and that you are unreliable and cannot be trusted to do what you say you are going to do.

Be organized and have a professional notepad on which to make notes. This will show the prospect that if you gain their business, you can be trusted to deliver superior service.

SET THE AGENDA:

Begin the appointment by setting the agenda. Tell the prospect what you are there to accomplish and how much time you will need. When you finish setting the agenda ask the prospect, "Does that sound all right?" This will gain the prospect's attention and let him know up front the amount of time he is investing in your appointment. Now stick to your agenda and stay within your stated time frame. How many times has someone asked for five minutes and taken thirty minutes? How does that make you feel? If you need thirty minutes, just ask for it.

ASK GOOD QUESTIONS:

You gain all the information you need just by asking good questions. Imagine you are a detective and gathering evidence. Have you ever known someone who loved to talk about himself or herself? We all know people like this. Well guess what, if all you do on your sales calls is talk about you and your company to your prospect, you are one of those people.

People hate to be sold, but they love to buy!
Jeffrey Gitomer

Take an interest in your prospect and their business. Have your questions prepared prior to the sales call, DON'T WING IT! Remember you are a professional sales representative so act like it!

Examples of good questions:
1) How long have you been with the company?
2) What do you like most about this company?
3) Are you in a competitive business?
4) What separates your company from the other companies in your industry?
5) Do you currently have a _____?
6) Were you involved in implementing the original ___ ___?
7) Why did you company start using a _____?
8) Is your current _____ meeting your original objectives?
9) Is your current _____ meeting your current needs?
10) If you could change one thing about your _____, what would it be?
11) Is there anyone beside you involved in the decision process?
12) How does your decision process work?
13) Who will sign the agreement to get the _____ started?

The purpose of asking questions is to determine who makes the decision, and how the decision process works. You are also determining the prospects needs, and discovering a buying motive or hot button. In addition, you need to discover any bias or potential objections that you can proactively address in your presentation.

Six reasons people buy
1) To make money, or to save money
2) Impulse or instant gratification
3) Save time, or convenience
4) Impress others, or increase status
5) Satisfy a need, or perceived need
6) Because everyone else is buying, or to conform

Six reasons people will buy from you:
1) You are there first (good timing)
2) Obligation
3) They like you
4) They trust you
5) You have the best price, or value
6) Your company provides the best product, or service

On the typical sales call you will probably have fifteen minutes to ask your prospect questions. In that time you will need to discover why the prospect will buy, make sure they like you, trust you, see your company and your company's services as the best in the industry, and provide these products and services at the best value. Oh, and by the way it won't hurt if you obligate the prospect and get there first!

Be sure to ask questions with a purpose. Do not waste your time or the prospect's time with idle talk without a purpose. Don't ask about the fish on the wall until after the sale is made! Time is what you exchange for money. The more effective you are with your time, the more sales calls you can make.

MORE SALES CALLS = MORE SALES = MORE MONEY = MORE FUN!

PRESENTATION SKILLS:

Presenting your company:

You will need to be able to demonstrate to the prospect beyond any reasonable doubt that your company is the company to do business with.

How do you do this? Have a professional presentation binder with credibility pieces, national references, and local references.

Remember you are paid to say the good things about your company and your prospect knows this. Show them what others say about your company. Practice your presentation and record it on videotape. Have top performing sales reps watch it and give you constructive criticism. Would you play on a team, or in a band, and expect to win without practice. It is the same in sales. Remember the better your skill, the more confidence you will have and the more you will enjoy what you do.

After hearing your presentation the prospect should say WOW!

Ways to add **WOW** to your presentation:

1) Videotape your service staff introducing themselves and stating their role in servicing the customer. Remind them to talk loud and smile. Catch them having fun.

2) Videotape testimonials of happy satisfied customers. What your customers say will mean much more than what you say. They now have recorders that will record

directly on a DVD and are ready for immediate use. Work smart! THIS WORKS! DO IT NOW!

3) Don't act and sound like every other sales rep your prospect sees. Average salespeople get average results, and average results will produce average pay.

Real Life Example:

Rick was calling on a prospect. After a fantastic presentation, Rick transitioned into a company introduction. After showing a couple of credibility pieces, Rick opened his binder to a picture of one of his customers that he had signed. He told the prospect that he could talk all day long about how great his company is but instead, he wanted the prospect to hear it for himself. At that point, Rick pulled out a tape player and played an audio interview of Rick and his customer (who was pictured on the credibility binder) talking about his company and their great service! After the first testimonial, Rick played two more interviews (with pictures) and trial closed on his company as a viable supplier for their program. It was incredible! **ARE YOUR PRESENTATIONS INCREDIBLE?**

Remember average pays average, and **INCREDIBLE PAYS INCREDIBLY!**

4) Use a nice pen and perfect the art of precision pointing. Precision pointing is done by looking at the chart or paper you are discussing and pointing above the word with your pen, and pressing down firmly to show confidence. Do not look at the prospect when presenting the information you want them to focus on, or they will be looking at you rather than the material. Look where you want them to look.

5) Put a Power Point presentation along with video taped references on a DVD and carry a small DVD player. Show this to your prospects. They will love it. Continue to add testimonials from your service partners and your customers.

6) Believe in your product and your company, or sell another product, or company.

IF YOU BELIEVE, THEY WILL BELIEVE. IF YOU DON'T BELIEVE, THEY WON'T BELIEVE EITHER.

Presenting Your Products:

You will now use the information that you gathered with your good business related questions. Sell benefits of your products and focus very little on the features. Present the products that address the needs of your prospect. Hopefully you discovered the prospect's buying motive, or hot button. Show the prospect how your products or services will help them make money, or save money. Use the names of current customers your prospect will recognize during your presentation of products. Let them read testimonial letters, and watch video taped testimonials during your presentation.

My brother John, who became wealthy as a 100% commissioned sales person says he always uses testimonials of at least twelve current customers when presenting his products and services. When your prospect sees others who have used your product, or service and made or saved money, the closing process is much easier. You can eliminate the fear of making a mistake. Try this-it works!

CLOSING:

You will notice the section on closing is a short section.

I have heard reps say they are strong at closing, and they have all sorts of fancy closes. If this fits your style and works for you, then do it. However, if you have done a great job asking questions, discovering a need, and presenting your products and services to the prospects needs, closing should be a smooth transition.

Closing is as simple as asking for the order. It can be as simple as saying, "Does this _____ sound like something that would benefit your company? Great! All we have to do is take the order and get your signature. Will that be all right?"

Remember to say this with confidence while smiling and nodding your head yes. Easy, right? The better you ask questions, present, and handle objections early, the easier closing will be.

Trial close throughout the sales process in order to remove any later objections. Use statements such as, "Does this sound like a _____that will benefit your company?" or "Can you see how our systems and procedures can eliminate your problems with _____?" How about the famous, "Does my company sound like the type of company that you would to do business with?" Use common sense and try to develop enough rapport with the prospect so your sales process seems almost conversational. When you believe in your company and your product, you should be excited when asking the prospect for their business. Let them know how much their account means to your and your company. ASK FOR THEIR BUSINESS!

HANDLING OBJECTIONS:

The better you are at asking questions and presenting, the fewer objections you will have. So if you are getting the same objections repeatedly on your appointments, don't necessarily work on handling these objections. You need to go back to your rapport building questions and presentation of company and products to see what could be causing the prospect's objections. Most likely you will need to make adjustments in your presentation.

For Example:

Your prospects are consistently objecting to signing a contract. Rather than work on handling this objection, go back and work on your presentation of your company, your products, and services. Add testimonial letters of satisfied customers the prospects will recognize, and you may even want to add their testimonials on videotape. I believe you will begin to see a great reduction in the number of prospects who object to signing a contract. Try this it works!

But be ready objections are buying signals.

Typical Objections:

1) I can't afford it.
2) Your price is too high.
3) I won't sign a contract.
4) I am happy with my current way of doing things.
5) Not now. I want to think about it. *
6) Check back with me in a few months. *
7) I have to talk it over with my partner. *
8) I have to talk to another supplier before I make my decision.

It will be up to you to ask good questions to overcome these objections. Whenever possible answer an objection with a question. Remember, the more you talk, the less likely you are to make the sale. However, I do want to help you with the four objections marked with an asterisk because I have discovered what I believe is the real objection, and I want to help you.

Objection #5) Not now, I want to think about it.

Ask the prospect what it is that most concerns them and be sure to address what they will be thinking about. If they have legitimate concerns you will need to address them before you leave the appointment, or you will not make the sale.

Objection #6) Check back in a few months.

This is most likely a no. The prospect just doesn't have the heart to say no to you. You should check back but do not get caught up thinking they are going to become a customer. I have seen sales reps get caught up in the check back routine. The money is in the new presentations. **Move on!**

Objection #7) I have to talk it over with my partner.

If you count on your prospect to sell the account for you, count on being disappointed. You do this for a living, and I think we are discovering that we are not real good at it. Just think how well your prospect will do with presenting your products and handling objections. You must get an appointment to come back and go through your full presentation again. Before you do this make sure your prospect would go along with your proposal if it were solely up to them. They may be attempting to give you a polite no. Can you believe anyone would do this? You better believe it! Some people just can't say no.

When you get an objection, do not take it personal. What the prospect is actually saying is, I do not see the value, I do not trust you (do you automatically trust sales people who call on you?), or I do not fully understand your proposition. In other words, something was lacking in your rapport building or presentation. Now is your chance to recover.

Remember, sales is a game of percentages. You will never sell every account that you call on. However, raising the percentage of accounts you close will affect your results dramatically.

Techniques to overcome objections:

1) Feel, Felt, Found: I understand how you FEEL. ABC Company FELT the same way. However when they FOUND that our service helps them increase employee morale, therefore increasing production, and reducing turnover, they were excited to have me come in and explain the program further to their employees.

2) The key to overcoming any objection is asking good questions. Remember that you are not unlike a trial attorney. First, you must isolate the objection to make sure it is the only objection.

Example:

Prospect: I can't afford it.

If money was no object, is this something you would like to do?

Prospect: Yes.

Would you have any other concerns?

Prospect: Well, I am not sure our employees would like the new _____anyway.

Are there any other concerns?

Prospect: No.

In other words, if I could show you how this program will actually be a money maker for your company just like it has for ABC Company and XYZ Company, and your employees approve and buy in, this is something you would like to implement?

Prospect: Yes, but how will your program make my company money?

So here is your big chance. Your assignment is to decide how your product can benefit the prospect, and why your company is the best at providing this product. In other words, you first have to get sold before you can persuade others.

DEVELOP A HOT PROSPECT LIST:

After you have presented to a prospect and they did not buy, however you believe they should and will buy within the next sixty days, you next want to put them on a list so you will not forget to close the business. We will call this your "Hot Prospect List". Keep track of the total volume of business on this list. You should have prospects signing with you from this list every week and should be adding new prospects to this list. You can't depend on luck. You need to work this list and continue to have great new presentations. Be sure to send them a professional thank you note. Tell them you enjoyed meeting with them and look forward to earning their business and providing them with legendary service. Be sure to sound professional, not just thanking them for seeing you. This makes you sound grateful just to have an appointment. Always make the impression that everyone buys from you.

EXAMPLE OF A "HOT PROSPECT LIST"

COMPANY	PHONE #	CONTACT	VOLUME
1.			
2.			
3.			
4.			
5.			
6.			
7.			
8.			
9.			
10.			
11.			
12.			
13.			
14.			
15.			

Total Volume in Hot Prospect List

The Hot Prospect list allows you to focus on work while at work and focus on home at home. You have your prospects out of your head and down on paper. You will not let prospects, "Fall through the cracks."

DEVELOP AN ACCOUNTS SOLD LIST:

Great! The process has worked! You found a prospect, gave a great opening statement, got the appointment, put full information in your day timer, arrived at the appointment on time, dressed for success, had a professional notepad to take notes, set the agenda, asked good business related questions, discovered a need, proved your company was the best to handle the clients needs, wowed the prospect with a great presentation of your products, asked for the business, handled their resistance, asked for the business again, and **made the sale!** Congratulations you can now put the account on the "Accounts Sold" list and **Go get another one!**

EXAMPLE OF AN "ACCOUNTS SOLD LIST"

COMPANY	PHONE #	VOLUME	YTD SOLD
1.			
2.			
3.			
4.			
5.			
6.			
7.			
8.			
9.			
10.			
11.			
12.			
13.			
14.			
15.			

TOTAL VOLUME SOLD

You can put your Hot Prospect list along with your Accounts Sold list and your day timer in a binder and create your own **Sales Rep Playbook**. Has someone ever told you "Just run the playbook", but you had no idea what the playbook was? Remember that you are responsible so create your own winning sales playbook! This will allow you to know the number of new presentations you need in order to make a sale. It will allow you to determine your closing ratio. You simply divide the number of accounts sold during a given time by the number of presentations you did during that time. When I was a sale rep I knew for every three presentations I would average one sale. I also knew my average size account and my average commission on that account. This will allow you to control your own destiny. You can be as successful and make as much money as you want.

The two ways to achieve your goals are:

1) Give more presentations. You may need five presentations to make a sale, however if you give twice as many presentations as I do each week you can still produce better results and make more money.

2) Improve your sales skills and effectiveness, and therefore, improve your closing ratio.

Remember that you could make even more money if you do both. **Work harder and smarter!**

THE "SYSTEM": I have used this system to become one of the top sales representatives for a Fortune 500 company. Maybe it will work for you.

1) Start every day with thirty minutes in a positive motivational book. This puts you in the right mind frame to have a successful day. By reading thirty minutes a day, in five years you will be an expert. Experts make six figures.

2) Minimum of fifteen cold calls per day. Thirty if you have no appointments. Cold call with a purpose, to get an appointment. Do not get in the habit of asking programmers are they happy. Just get the appointment.

3) Fifteen new presentations to decision-makers every week. To get appointments you must be good on the phone and when cold calling. Develop a great opening statement and use it!

4) Skills. This could be #1 on the list. We need to get better every day. Practice, Practice, Practice!

   A) **Introduction:** Know how to introduce yourself. Have an opening statement and use it. Better introduction = More appointments = more sales = more money = more fun!

   B) **Probe and Build Rapport:** Ask good questions. Read Jeffrey Gitomer's *Sales Bible* or Hal Becker's *Can I Have Five Minutes of Your Time?* Learn to develop good questions with a purpose. Not "I see that fish on the wall. Do you fish?" Don't waste time! Time is money!

   C) **Introducing and Presenting your Company:** You need a professional binder and good presentation skills. It should be full of credibility pieces and reference letters that prove you are the best company. Be organized and neat. Have a great presentation you use every time. Don't "wing it!"

D) Closing and Handling Objections: Better questions and presentation skill = fewer objections but be ready. Objections are buying signals. Read sales books, practice. Learn how to handle objections. Remember, go back and practice on your questions and presentation skills and you will get fewer objections.

5) Identify and get to know twenty-five target accounts. Be creative and seed mail them every quarter. Think long term, develop a relationship. Sell some now, and sell more later.

6) Ask each appointment for at least three references.

7) Go to the City Hall in your territory once a month and get a copy of new business licenses. Get there first. Work smart.

Have a good follow-up system. Keep every business card. Make notes on them. Keep them in a binder. Use the sold ones as references and in a separate binder keep the not yet sold cards. Organize them and develop a database using a card scan. If your company has a database of prospects be sure to keep it current.

CHAPTER FIVE
LEAD AND DUPLICATE YOURSELF;
CREATE!

Leadership is a choice
Dr. Stephen Covey

Notice the word **CREATE** in the title. What does that mean to you? I want you to think about this with everything you do as the leader. A temptation you will have as a leader is to **REACT**. Do not get into the reaction business. Get into the CREATION business! Yes, you will have non-performers and difficult weeks. You will have results that are below standards that you have to explain to your boss, but if you get into the reaction business, you will lose the game. To win the game and enjoy your role as a leader, your task is to **CREATE** an environment that is conducive to peak performance.

When your team's performance is below expectations, you must reexamine yourself based on the four keys we will talk about in this chapter. Ask yourself, did I do a good job in my hiring process? If so, did I do a good job in my training process? If so, are there barriers to the partner's success that need removing? And finally, is our environment a fun one?

Notice again, everything goes back to you as the leader, you are responsible. When things go well you are responsible. When things don't go well you are responsible. Get it? By now if you haven't bought into the fact that you need to become a student of sales and leadership, Darn it! Buy in! Are you telling me you have no room for improvement! Horse poop! *"Leaders are readers".* I did not make that quote up, it has been around for years and it is a fact.

Let me make the point this way. You get to pick a team. The first team is a team of readers. They love reading Brian Tracy, Jeffrey Gitomer, and books by every successful sales mentor they can find. They not only read, but they share information and techniques. The second team does not read or buy into self—improvement. There is no other difference in the two teams. Keep in mind they are new to your company with no results to measure at this point. Which team do you want? Get the picture? You are the leader, so lead by example and read!

I have known many leaders who were not managers, and I have known many managers who were not leaders. In order to get a team to produce great results you must be a great leader. Leaders operate with integrity. It takes years to build trust and integrity, but it can be lost in seconds. Your reputation is the most important thing you have. Guard it carefully. Do not go out drinking and partying with your reps. You can enjoy a drink, but stay professional at all times. Never use foul language when you are with subordinates or prospects, even if they do. A mentor of mine early in my career suggested that I ask myself this question when making a decision, "Can it help you? "Can it hurt you?" If the action will only help you, then do it. If it could hurt you or your reputation then don't.

You must have a clear understanding of your company's

vision and convey this to your team. Understanding that our job is to help the company achieve the company's objectives, while at the same time realizing that our direct reports have their own goals. We must help them get what they want. You must continually sell them on the fact that they can get everything they desire from life right here at your company. All they need to do is become valuable and help the company achieve its objectives.

KEYS TO BUILDING A GREAT TEAM:

KEY I: HIRING

The most important decision we make as leaders is whom we bring on our team. I heard a football coach say once, *"You can't teach speed"*. Part of your goal should be to have a highly talented, motivated team of partners who are compatible with your company's culture and enjoy what they do.

As we discussed our responsibility as leaders of a team is to create an environment that is conducive to peak performance. Winners want to associate with winners. The old saying, *"One apple can spoil the whole bunch"* holds true. Just think what two or three bad apples can do! You are looking for people who fit your culture.

When you meet the candidate they should speak in a professional manner, be dressed professionally, and be respectful, courteous, and enthusiastic! When you meet the candidate be aware of your first impression of them and remember that this is the same first impression the prospect will have of them. Is it a great one? Do they **walk fast, talk loud, and smile?** By the way, is the above a description of you? If not, it better be from now on. Remember, walk the talk! You may get by being less than great in the next three key areas, but you cannot build a great team unless you get great at hiring. Find someone that has an opinion you respect and have them involved in the hiring process. You may be desperate, so have someone who is not desperate share with you his or her honest opinion. Read books on hiring, watch others who have hired great people interview, and get their advice.

Get better at recruiting so that you have more candidates to choose from. Go to job fairs. Consult with leaders who have built great teams and get recruiting ideas. Remember good people will attract good people so when you hire and train great people, they will be your best resource for candidates. It will get easier, just like in sales, your first year as a leader will be the hardest you ever work and the least amount of money you ever make as a leader. So do it right and you will love it!

KEY II: TRAINING

The more skilled sales reps become, the more they will enjoy their work. Your people will love what they do and produce unbelievable results if you help them get good! When a new partner joins your team your must put them through a thorough training program. Do not cut the process short. New partners need to work in every department in your organization and understand the new account process, as well as ride with the sales reps. Remember, there is no going back, when a rep is new, build a solid foundation for their future. This will help them better serve the prospect, sell more business, and sell better business in the future. This will also help them feel and become part of the team.

One of the biggest factors in creating a positive environment that is conducive to peak performance will be your sales meeting.

How to conduct an effective sales meeting:

Remember: Sales meetings should be fun. The reps should look forward to the sales meeting. They should be conducted Monday mornings. I suggest 7:45 am. They should last one hour and no more. THIS IS YOUR TIME TO CREATE A GREAT WEEK! So you won't have to react to a less than great week.

Here is an agenda for a fun high impact meeting:

A game of 7's (5 to 10 minutes):

Everyone stands up and gets in a circle. You start the game by saying ONE! Say the number while smiling and talking loud. The rep to your left says TWO! And everyone counts off until you get to a seven, a number with a seven in it, or a multiple of seven. When you get to one of these numbers the rep claps and the rotation reverses. If you or a rep says the number rather than clap that person sits down and is out of the game. The game continues until you have a winner. The key is to laugh, yell the number, get fired up, and have fun. You can have everyone put in a dollar, and the winner gets the money. This is a great game for sales teams because the more the reps practice the game, the better they will get, and the more money they will make. It is the same with sales skills.

Good News (5 minutes):

Go around the room and each rep tells of something good and business related that happened last week.

Information (5 to 10 minutes):

The sales manager or sales support leader gives information necessary for the sales team. Business trends, sales contest, new product information etc.

Training (10 minutes):

This is just a quick fun check up on the skills the reps have been working on in the training meetings and on their own. A fun game is to throw a tennis ball to a rep and have them give their opening statement, or another sales related skill. They then can throw the ball to a teammate who is then asked to handle an objection etc.

Motivation (20 minutes):

It is true that if you hired the right person they will be self-motivated. However, everyone can use a little inspiration to start the week. This is a great chance to remind everyone how he or she can get everything wanted out of life by becoming a real professional at the chosen profession of sales. Sell the grand vision of what we are going to become. Keep the team focused on the routine that will help them achieve their goals. The sales manager or rep can get up and inspire the team with something they have read in a sales related book.

Close on a positive note (2 to 5 minutes):

Make a challenge to your team and remind them what is in it for them when they achieve their goals. A successful career is just a series of successful days. So go have five great days!

The purpose of the sales meeting is to motivate the reps on the value of becoming a professional sales rep. What it will mean to their careers. You also sell them on the fact that they can get everything they want from life right here at your company. Do you believe this? If not go work for another company! As I stated in the first part of this book, most often, *"The change we need is within ourselves."* We need a change of attitude and skills. If your team is great it is because you are great, if your team stinks it is because you stink!

The four keys to developing a great team are hiring, training, removing barriers/accountability, and having fun. Look at these key areas and evaluate yourself. There you will find the answer. Another major factor in creating a positive environment that is conducive to peak performance will be your training meeting. Training meetings should be used to inspect what you expect. This is a time for the reps to show off what they have been practicing on their own time. If this is the only time they practice they will not be successful. Who is at fault if this happens? You guessed it! You are! Did you make a mistake in hiring? Did you not sell them on the value of practice? Get back at it and make the sale! If they still do not practice, you must now document the rep based on performance. When you get good at leading and creating, you will seldom need to document performance. You will be too busy giving recognition!

How to conduct an effective sales training meeting:

Focus on the key steps of the sales process: Remember to Coach, Teach, Role Play, and Have Fun! When your reps are highly skilled in the six steps of the sales process, they will enjoy their work.

Remember, high skill = high morale = high productivity.

Step 1) Introduction: In order to secure quality appointments, the reps must have an opening statement that will create interest and credibility.

Step 2) Build Rapport/Probe: In order to determine the prospect's needs, the rep's ability to ask good questions is vital.

Steps 3/4) Introduce the Company/Present Products: The ability for your reps to show your company as the best company is vital to their success.

Steps 5/6) Close and Handle Objections: Better questions and presentations = fewer objections. Be sure the reps trial close throughout the process. A fun way to conduct a training meeting is to have a sales presentation contest.

Give each rep 20 minutes to give their presentation. Get the presentation on videotape.

Award prizes and make it fun. Give them three or four weeks of advanced notice so they will practice, and get unbiased judges from the service department. You can review the videotaped presentations with the rep as a coaching tool. Remember, improve skill and you will improve morale and productivity. It is that simple.

I have a sales associate on my team that was really struggling. Her average was well below expectations. She had gone from an enthusiastic beginner to a disillusioned learner really fast. Her skill was low so she dreaded making sales calls. Who wants to do something they are not good at? It was a reflection of my training program. However, if you hire the right people, they will find a way to overcome poor coaching.

Beth Davis is doing just that. She decided that in order to give a great presentation she would need a script. So Beth wrote a sales presentation script and practiced it on videotape until she had a great presentation. As a result, the next training meeting Beth blew us away with her presentation. She now enjoys her work because she is good at it. Beth is now exceeding her quota with her new skill and continues to improve. As her skill continues to improve she will enjoy her work even more. As a result she will make more money, and move up in the company.

KEY III: REMOVE BARRIERS/ACCOUNTABILITY

Once your partners are trained and have reached, or had adequate opportunity to reach the skill level to succeed, you need to hold them accountable. Keep in mind that if the sales rep has good skill and a good routine they will produce results. So if the results are not there, you know they are not running the routine. As we continue to stress, there could be several reasons:

1)   You hired the wrong person
2)   Your training program is lacking
3)   There are barriers to the sales reps success
4)   The environment is not fun

Notice once again, with great benefit, all the factors go back to you, the leader. If you hired the wrong person, then you need to part ways as quickly as possible. If your training program is lacking, you probably have more than one sales rep that is struggling. If there are barriers to your sales reps' success, you need to discover them and remove them immediately. If they are not having fun you need to create a fun environment. Remember your job as the leader is to create an environment where the high achievers are happy, and the underachievers are not.

KEY IV: HAVE FUN

Now this should be self explanatory, but I just can't believe how many sales environments are not fun. Let's have fun! When your team wins, celebrate together! When you don't, get back to the basics and improve your skill, trust the routine, and, Act as if it were impossible to fail!

One who has mastered the art of living simply pursues his vision of excellence at whatever he does, leaving others to decide whether he is working or playing.
James Michener

I would like to share with you my original Game Plan for

the sales leadership role in the Chattanooga market. I hope it serves you as well as it has me.

MANAGEMENT SYSTEM

1) Hire sales professionals with high goals and help them achieve them.

2) Monday Meetings—7:45 to 8:45am. Never more than one hour.

   Agenda:

   7's   (5 to 10 minutes)

   Good News   (5 minutes)

   Information   (5 to 10 minutes)

   Training   (10 minutes)

   Motivation   (20 minutes)

   Close on a Positive Note   (2 minutes)

3) Ride with new sales reps.

   A) Inspect what you expect. (This means observe skill and routine)

   B) Observe. Do not interfere on appointments.

   C) At the end of the day, tell what was good and offer what can be done to improve results.

4) Reps sell prospects on the value of your company's services and products to their business. As the leader, continually sell reps on the value of your company to their careers and families. A good leader helps his or her people get what they want from their careers.

5) The team will be professional and always looking to improve their sales skills.

6) Strive to maintain a positive attitude and always cheer for teammates.

7) Plan your work and work your plan. Have a strategy and utilize time proven methods to ensure success.

A) Phone blocks
B) 15 to 30 cold calls per day
C) 15 set appointments per week
D) Be a real professional at the basics

8) We will WORK HARD AND HAVE FUN!

Your plan will most likely not be the same as mine. But remember, **if you fail to plan, you plan to fail**. Have a good game plan, and stick with it!

In conclusion, I leave you with a quote from Cintas Corporation founder Dick Farmer at the Cintas Annual Meeting in 1999:

We are fortunate to have an abundance of strong-willed leaders—people who can stand up to the tough decisions. But good fortune really has nothing to do with it.

We have high standards when we select new people. We go after the best people. We train them to be leaders in the Cintas Corporation mold. They are given responsibilities and opportunities very early in their careers—unheard of in other business organizations.

We place our new people in positions where expectations are very high, and we encourage them to be innovative in ways that will lead them to success. And you know…they find ways to achieve the expectations and to be successful.

Before long, they become supremely confident, because they have had experience in scaling mountains that seem not climbable to most people. Then exciting things start to happen.

Our new leaders develop a "can do attitude" that is contagious! The leaders who live up to our values and standards become such a powerful, dynamic force; they inspire every partner in their circle of influence.

It is up to you to develop the leaders of tomorrow. You have more opportunities today than ever before. This is an awesome responsibility so take it seriously.

Lead by example and get into self-improvement and inspire everyone in your circle of influence to get into self-improvement.

Dave Prebenda, who was just one month older than me, died at the age of 32. He left behind his wife and two children. I feel his presence watching over me often and believe he has in some way helped guide my career.

I hope I have inspired you to give it 100% in your sales career. Remember that life is short, so have fun and go for it.

BURN YOUR BOATS!

WE WIN OR WE PERISH!

CREDITS

I would like to thank and acknowledge everyone who has influenced my life. Few if any ideas contained in this book are my own. Some ideas I know where they originated and gave credit. Some ideas I do not know their origin.

For example, as stated in the beginning of this book, I had a wonderful childhood. I was blessed with two loving parents who cared about their children. I was taught priceless values, many by observing my parents. They deserve the credit for much of this book.

I would like to thank God for blessing me with the life that I have, and I pray and encourage each of you to pray for those who are born into less than ideal circumstances. Let's vow to do something to help these children.

I would like to thank my beautiful wife Laura for all of her love and support. Without her, this book would not have been possible.

Next, I would like to thank Richard T. Farmer the founder of Cintas Corporation. This company has a corporate culture and values that will make any person better. Many ideas from my philosophy on leadership to my sales approach came from my being in such a positive, high trust sales environment.

The book was dedicated to Dick Surdykowski, Mark Biasucci, and Dave Prebenda the partners who thought enough of me to hire me when I really needed a job.

I would like to thank and recommend for your reading

the countless authors that have influenced me in ways I can never repay. Starting with Jeffrey Gitomer who sent me a copy of Earl Nightingale's, *The Strangest Secret* when I became the leader of a sales team in Chattanooga, Tennessee. I would recommend everyone read these authors: Napoleon Hill, *Think and Grow Rich*, Brian Tracy, *The 100 Absolutely Unbreakable Laws of Business Success*, and *How to be a Sales Superstar*, he has many more all of which are great.

I would also like to thank Dr. Stephen R. Covey for his book, *The 8th Habit*, and *The 7 Habits of Highly Effective People*. Hal Becker for his book, *Can I Have 5 Minutes of Your Time?"* Steve Chandler for his book, *100 Ways to Motivate Others*. There are many more, but these are the books that have inspired me the most.

I encourage you to make self-improvement a priority in your life. At one time, I thought it was not for me, and now I have a higher enjoyment for life that I could ever have imagined.

2292585

Made in the USA